It's My State!

DELAWARE

The First State

David King, Brian Fitzgerald, and Kerry Jones Waring

Cavendish
Square

New York

Published in 2015 by Cavendish Square Publishing, LLC
243 5th Avenue, Suite 136, New York, NY 10016

Website: cavendishsq.com

CPSIA Compliance Information: Batch #WW15CSQ

All websites were available and accurate when this book was sent to press.

Library of Congress Cataloging-in-Publication Data

King, David C.
Delaware / David King, Brian Fitzgerald, Kerry Waring. — Third Edition.
pages cm. — (It's my state)
Includes index.
ISBN 978-1-50260-009-7 (library binding) ISBN 978-1-50260-010-3 (ebook)
1. Delaware—Juvenile literature. I. Fitzgerald, Brian, 1972- II. Waring, Kerry Jones. III. Title.

F164.3.K56 2015
975.1—dc23

2014024972

Editor: Fletcher Doyle
Senior Copy Editor: Wendy A. Reynolds
Art Director: Jeffrey Talbot
Designer: Joseph Macri
Senior Production Manager: Jennifer Ryder-Talbot
Production Editor: David McNamara
Photo Research by J8 media

DELAWARE ★ ★ ★ ★

CONTENTS

A QUICK LOOK AT

★ State Flower: Peach Blossom

In the late 1800s, peaches were a booming industry in Delaware, but a disease called the peach yellows wiped them out. The peach blossom was adopted as the state flower in 1895 and remains a symbol of Delaware's proud farming history.

★ State Insect: Ladybug

In 1974, a second grade class from a school in Milford led the effort to make the ladybug the state insect. The state legislature approved the idea in April of that year. Five other states have since adopted the ladybug as their official insect.

★ State Tree: American Holly

The American holly tree has long been a symbol of the Christmas season. The evergreen tree is known for its thick, pointy leaves and bright red berries. American hollies grow as tall as 60 feet (18 meters).

DELAWARE

★ State Beverage: Milk

Milk was adopted as the official state beverage in 1983. Dairy farms have always been important to Delaware's economy. Milk from Delaware's cows is sold throughout Delaware and to other states and is used in products such as cheese, ice cream, and butter.

★ State Fossil: Belemnite

Named Delaware's state fossil in 1996, belemnites are extinct sea creatures that were related to certain types of modern-day squid. In Delaware, **belemnite** fossils are most often found along the Chesapeake and Delaware Canal.

★ State Marine Animal: Horseshoe Crab

Each spring, hundreds of thousands of horseshoe crabs deposit their eggs on the sandy shores of Delaware Bay. Horseshoe crabs are not true crabs—they are more closely related to scorpions or spiders. The horseshoe crab became Delaware's state marine animal in 2002.

Cape Henlopen State Park near Lewes provides access to the Atlantic Ocean and to Delaware Bay.

The First State

With a land area of just 1,982 square miles (5,133 square kilometers), Delaware is the second-smallest state in the U.S. Only Rhode Island is smaller. In fact, nearby Philadelphia, Pennsylvania, is one of several U.S. cities that have more people than all of Delaware. However, there is one list on which Delaware will always be number one.

On December 7, 1787, Delaware became the first of the thirteen original American states to ratify, or approve, the U.S. Constitution. That's why Delaware's nickname is "the First State."

Delaware may be small, but its history is packed with colorful events. There are reminders of America's past all over the state. Delaware is a state of great natural beauty, with countless opportunities for work and for recreation. Proud Delawareans agree with the state slogan: "It's good being first."

The Landscape

Delaware is just 96 miles (155 km) long, and it is very narrow. The state is only 35 miles (56 km) across at its widest point. Delaware has only three counties, the fewest of any state. Roughly two-thirds of the people live in the northern county of New Castle.

Wilmington is a center for big business.

Wilmington, the largest city in Delaware, is in New Castle County. Kent County in central Delaware is home to Dover, the state capital. Kent and the southernmost county of Sussex are more rural and less heavily populated.

Most of Delaware sits on a long **peninsula**—a stretch of land that is surrounded by water on three sides. This area, called the Delmarva Peninsula, also includes parts of Maryland and Virginia. The peninsula's name is a combination of the names of those three states. The Delaware River, Delaware Bay, and the Atlantic Ocean border the eastern side of the peninsula. Chesapeake Bay lies on its western side.

Delaware has only two geographic regions. Most of the state is part of the Atlantic Coastal Plain—a narrow belt of lowland that extends from New York to Florida. Delaware is the lowest state in the country. The average elevation is just 60 feet (18 m) above sea level.

Delaware Borders	
North:	Pennsylvania
South:	Maryland
East:	New Jersey
	Delaware Bay
	Atlantic Ocean
West:	Maryland

A narrow strip of land in northern Delaware is part of a region called the Piedmont. This area of gently rolling hills lies between the Atlantic Coastal Plain and the Appalachian Mountains. Delaware's highest point is found in this area, very close to the Pennsylvania border. A spot near Ebright Road in New Castle County rises 448 feet (137 m) above sea level. Delaware's highest point is actually much lower than the lowest point in many other states.

The marshy land in the southern part of the state forms the famous Great Cypress Swamp. The 30,000-acre (12,140-hectare) swamp is also known as the Great Pocomoke Swamp.

Water Tour

Delaware has 381 miles (613 km) of shoreline—a surprising amount for such a small state. Much of the coast borders Delaware Bay. This area has many shallow coves, sandy beaches, and marshy areas.

Delaware meets the Atlantic Ocean on the eastern edge of Sussex County. The sandy ocean coastline stretches 28 miles (45 km), from the Maryland border in the south to Cape Henlopen at the mouth of Delaware Bay. Rehoboth Beach and Bethany Beach are

People who visit Rehoboth Beach find activities that provide both recreation and relaxation.

NEW CASTLE

KENT

SUSSEX

Kent County	162,310
New Castle County	538,479
Sussex County	197,145

Source: U.S. Bureau of the Census, 2010

The many bodies of water in Delaware allow for many different kinds of fun.

The Chesapeake and Delaware Canal was built to connect Delaware Bay and Chesapeake Bay.

two of Delaware's most popular tourist destinations. A large part of this coastal area is a low sand bar that separates the ocean from the Rehoboth and Indian River bays.

Many small islands dot the coastline. The largest are Pea Patch Island and Reedy Island in the Delaware River. Pea Patch Island is home to Fort Delaware State Park. During the Civil War (1861–1865), the fort was used as a prison. Fenwick Island is near the state's southern border. It is a busy vacation spot during the summer.

A low sandy ridge extends north and south through the state just inside Delaware's western border. This ridge is the edge of one of the state's watersheds (land areas draining into bodies of water). The state's rivers flow either east into the Delaware River or Delaware Bay, or west into Chesapeake Bay. The Delaware River starts in New York State and flows south for more than 300 miles (483 km) before emptying into Delaware Bay. The river is one of the key shipping routes on the East Coast. A human-made waterway— the Chesapeake and Delaware Canal—cuts across the state just south of Wilmington. The canal connects Delaware Bay and Chesapeake Bay. These waterways played a vital role in Delaware's economic development by linking the state with major cities, especially Philadelphia and Baltimore.

Climate

Delaware has a moderate climate. Summers in most of the state are humid, with temperatures averaging between 70 and 80 degrees Fahrenheit (21 to 27 degrees Celsius). Ocean breezes make coastal areas a little cooler than the rest of the state. As summer turns to fall, leaves on trees begin to change colors. Residents and visitors alike enjoy the cooler weather and vivid colors of fall.

Winters in the First State are not as harsh as winters in more northern states. The mountainous regions of Pennsylvania block cold northwestern winds from hitting Delaware. The average winter temperature is about 36°F (2°C). Warm ocean currents keep coastal areas warmer than inland areas. The amount of snowfall varies from the north to the south. Wilmington gets about 20 inches (51 centimeters) of snow each year. Towns in Sussex County often get far less.

Delaware's beauty is reflected in the colors of the fall foliage.

★10 KEY SITES★ ★ ★

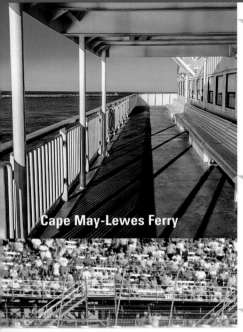

Cape May-Lewes Ferry

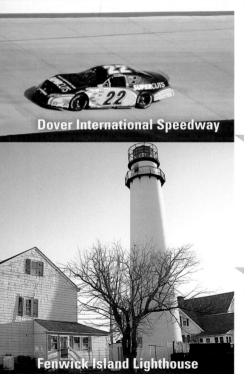

Dover International Speedway

Fenwick Island Lighthouse

1. Cape May-Lewes Ferry

This ferry has been cruising the Delaware River for more than fifty years, giving countless passengers an ideal view of the state's scenic waterfront locations. Riders can journey to several locations between New Jersey and Delaware, and enjoy special events such as onboard music programs.

2. Delaware Sports Museum and Hall of Fame

The Delaware Sports Museum and Hall of Fame honors and recognizes outstanding athletes from Delaware. The museum is located at Daniel S. Frawley Stadium in Wilmington, the home field for the city's minor league baseball team, the Blue Rocks.

3. Delaware AeroSpace Education Foundation Academy

Since 1990, the DASEF Academy in Smyrna has provided hands-on training and experience for young people, including programs that incorporate science, technology, engineering, and mathematics to encourage them to work in these areas as adults.

4. Dover International Speedway

Since opening in 1969, this well-known racetrack in Dover has hosted many important events, including two NASCAR races annually and the IndyCar series. The "Monster Mile" can hold up to 135,000 people in its stands.

5. Fenwick Island Lighthouse

This lighthouse was constructed in 1859 to help guide ships passing by Fenwick Island, located at the southern border of Delaware. The U.S. government paid resident Mary Hall just $50 for the land that would hold the lighthouse.

DELAWARE ★ ★ ★ ★

6. Fort Delaware State Park

Originally built to protect the ports of Wilmington and Philadelphia, Fort Delaware later housed Confederate prisoners during the Civil War. Today, visitors to the fort can experience history firsthand with the help of costumed interpreters and hands-on colonial activities.

7. The Grand Opera House

Opened in 1871, the Grand, as it is called, was restored to its original glory in the 1970s. Today, the Delaware Symphony, Opera Delaware, and First State Ballet Theater call the Grand home.

8. John Dickinson Plantation

John Dickinson was one of the founding fathers of the United States and a signer of the U.S. Constitution. Called "the Penman of the Revolution," his stately Dover home is now a museum.

9. New Castle Historical Society

This organization operates three museums in New Castle: the Amstel House, the Dutch House, and the Old Library Museum. Touring these museums will give you a glimpse at those who helped shape its culture, from Dutch laborers to British colonial governors.

10. Rehoboth Beach

Part of the Delaware Beaches cluster on the state's coastline, Rehoboth is known for its clean water and busy boardwalk. While the official population is just over 1,300 residents, it can grow to more than twenty-five thousand people during the summer.

Fort Delaware

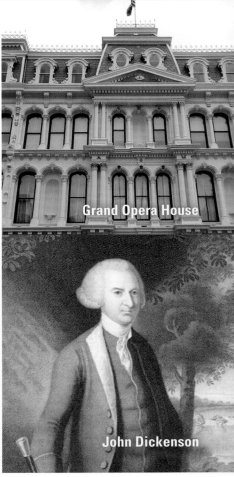
Grand Opera House

John Dickenson

Azaleas and other flowering plants decorate Delaware in the spring and summer.

Plant and Animal Life

About 30 percent of Delaware is covered by forests. Delaware and the whole Delmarva Peninsula are in a zone that includes both northern and southern plant life. Trees common to northern states are abundant, including oak, maple, hickory, and poplar. Trees that are found mainly in southern states, such as bald cypress, sweet gum, and loblolly pine, also thrive in Delaware.

From March to October, Delaware's level fields and meadows seem to be carpeted in wildflowers. The display begins in late winter with the first blossoming of crocuses and violets and extends through the asters and mums of late autumn. A number of flowering plants grow throughout spring and summer, including azaleas, morning glories, trumpet vines, and butterfly weeds. Water lilies and floating hearts add color to the many ponds, while pink and white hibiscus dot the marshy areas. Some swampland is almost impassable because of the thickets of wild blueberry and cranberry.

Delaware also has an abundance of wildlife. Its largest wild animal is deer. Others include rabbits, minks, otters, both red and gray foxes, muskrats, and raccoons. Diamondback terrapin live in marshy areas near the coast, and snapping turtles are common in and around swamps. Amphibians such as frogs, toads, and salamanders also live in the damp areas around water or on wet forest floors. You are never far from water in Delaware—whether it's the ocean, Delaware Bay, the many rivers and streams, or the state's fifty small lakes and ponds.

Bird watching is a favorite pastime for many in Delaware. More than 275 bird species have been identified within Bombay Hook National Wildlife Refuge on the shore of Delaware Bay. This amazing number includes songbirds, such as blue jays, robins, and cardinals. Shorebirds, such as herons and egrets, and a variety of ducks can also be found on its marshy shores. Each spring, the 16,000-acre (6,475-ha) refuge is a stopping point for migrating shorebirds. Up to one million birds feed along the shores of the bay before continuing their journey north. Similarly, the dunes of Fenwick Island State Park are popular for observing black skimmers, osprey, and piping plovers.

The salt water of Delaware Bay and the Atlantic Ocean, along with the many sources of fresh water, provide a great variety of fish. Many people enjoy surf fishing on the Atlantic beaches or taking chartered boats to search for flounder, rockfish, and weakfish. Closer to shore, the coastal waters provide sea trout, shad, and striped bass. Clamming and crabbing are also popular around Delaware Bay. Freshwater fish in rivers and ponds include bluegill, perch, and catfish.

Caring for the Environment

Lawmakers in Delaware have taken steps to preserve the state's environment and natural resources. By the 1970s, the growth of Delaware's cities and suburbs and the increase in factories and motor vehicles were filling the air with a yellowish haze. In the waterways, the harvest of fish and shellfish dropped off so sharply that many commercial fishers were forced out of the trade.

For many species of birds, Delaware is a seasonal or permanent home.

Volunteers patrol a Delaware beach for trash.

The Delaware state government passed several laws to reverse these trends. Delaware became one of the first states to establish a department of natural resources and environmental control. In 1971, the Coastal Zone Act stopped the building of any industrial plants along the state's coast.

Despite these efforts, the quality of air and water continued to decline. A government study in 1989 showed that 63 percent of Delaware's lakes, rivers, and streams were not safe for fishing or swimming. Eighty percent of the state's people lived in areas where the air did not meet federal standards.

Delawareans and their state officials have worked hard to reduce pollution. Special "action teams" work to clean up the state's waterways. By using these teams, the government is not tackling these problems alone. The state environmental agency has asked citizens to get involved by studying the sources of pollution and coming up with strategies to reduce pollution in the state's waterways. Government agencies also closely monitor air quality around the state. Strict laws have been passed to correct and regulate a variety of environmental problems.

Delawareans are also concerned about **global warming**—the slow increase in worldwide temperatures. One effect of global warming is rising sea levels. This could have a big impact on the wildlife, people, homes, and businesses in coastal areas of Delaware. The state is exploring ways

Gem of a Nickname

Thomas Jefferson gave Delaware the nickname "the diamond state," according to legend, because its strategic location on the Eastern Seaboard made it a "jewel" among states.

to reduce the use of the fossil fuels. Burning fossil fuels, such as coal, creates energy to produce electricity, but it also contributes to global warming. "Clean" energy sources, such as wind and solar power, are better for the environment.

Delaware's efforts to expand use of green energy have been noticed. The state had 29 times more solar installations in 2014 than it did in 2008. It was seventh nationally in solar installations per capita. From 2008 to 2014, it increased its solar capacity from two megawatts to fifty-nine megawatts to become a national leader in solar energy.

The Delaware Electric Cooperative's Bruce A. Henry Solar Energy Farm, which is close to Georgetown, was completed in the summer of 2013. It cost $14 million. There are sixteen thousand solar panels at the 20-acre facility, which produces enough energy to power 500 rural Sussex homes.

In the summer of 2014, the state created a Green Energy Fund to encourage people to install small-scale solar panel systems. The fund will also increase incentives for people to use more geothermal solar hot water systems to heat their homes.

Delaware encourages young people to get involved in helping the environment. The Young Environmentalist of the Year awards honor students who have worked to protect, restore, or improve the state's natural wonders. Any Delaware student can participate. To find out more, visit: www.dnrec.delaware.gov/Admin/Pages/YoungEnv.aspx.

Saltwater and freshwater fish are available in Delaware's waters.

Bald Cypress

Diamondback Terrapin

Least Tern

1. Bald Cypress

Common in the swamps of the Southeast, bald cypress trees are not found farther north than Delaware's Great Cypress Swamp. The cypress is easy to identify by the bald "knees" that grow from its roots and stick out of the water.

2. Beach Plum

In early autumn, you might spot a few beach visitors picking the beach plums that grow in abundance on low bushes in the sand dunes. The bright blossoms of spring turn into a small, tart fruit that can be made into a thick, tasty jam.

3. Diamondback Terrapin

Diamondback terrapins are medium-size turtles common in the marshes near Delaware's long beachfront. They get their name from the shape of the raised plates on their shells. A female's shell can measure up to 9 inches (23 cm).

4. Least Tern

Least terns are members of the gull family, but they are smaller and more graceful than seagulls. The terns' small size led to their name—the least of the terns. The terns migrate to Delaware Bay in mid-April to feast on horseshoe crab eggs.

5. Muskrat

Muskrats look very much like small beavers. A muskrat has brown fur, slightly webbed feet, and a broad, flat tail. Muskrats are found throughout Delaware's marshlands and ponds. Some Delawareans consider muskrat to be a tasty meal.

DELAWARE ★ ★ ★ ★

6. Sweet Golden Rod

Also known as "solidago odora," sweet golden rod was made the official state herb of Delaware in 1996. The plant can be found in many places throughout the state, especially areas near the ocean or marshes.

7. Tiger Swallowtail

Tiger swallowtails are black-and-yellow butterflies that can be found in Delaware's fields and trees from May through August. The tiger swallowtail was declared the state butterfly in 1999. Before they become butterflies, tiger swallowtails move around as green caterpillars with bright eyespots.

8. Wild Geranium

Wild geranium is one type of many beautiful wildflowers that grow in Delaware. The wild geranium is a **perennial**, meaning the same plant will grow again each spring. The color of its flowers ranges from pink to purple.

9. Shortnose Sturgeon

The Delaware River is an important habitat for this endangered species—meaning there are not many of these fish left in the world. Sturgeon are often called living fossils because they are among the oldest kind of bony fish.

10. Yellow Trout Lily

This flowering plant grows in colonies, or clusters, that continue to grow for a very long time. It gets its name from its gray-green leaves, which some say resemble the coloring of a fish called brook trout.

Tiger Swallowtail

Shortnose Sturgeon

Yellow Trout Lily

A replica of the Dutch-built *Kalmar Nyckel*, which brought the first European settlers to Delaware, can be toured in Wilmington.

From the Beginning

History seems to be everywhere in Delaware. In one small town after another, you can find carefully preserved village greens, old mills with stone grinding wheels, and even some roads still paved with cobblestones. The influence of the state's Native American history is easy to spot in many places in southern Sussex County. Delawareans are proud of these reminders of the past and they work hard to preserve and protect that heritage.

Under Four Flags

British explorer Henry Hudson became the first European to visit the area in 1609. He had been hired by the Dutch East India Company to find a route to the Far East. Hudson briefly sailed into Delaware Bay before turning back and heading farther north up the Atlantic coast. He instead explored the river in New York that is now named for him.

The name Delaware was given to the bay and the river in 1610. English sea captain Samuel Argall named the bodies of water in honor of Sir Thomas West, Lord De la Warr. West was serving as governor of Virginia—the only English colony in North America at the time. The name was later applied to the land on the western side of Delaware Bay and the southern end of the Delaware River.

Swedes, shown landing in the 1600s, were among the first Europeans to arrive in Delaware.

Residents of the present-day town of Lewes often call their town "the first town in the first state." It was there that a group of Dutch settlers had hoped to start a colony in 1631. That early settlement was named Zwaanendael, which meant "valley of the swans." The settlement lasted less than two years. After a misunderstanding over stolen property, the Lenape destroyed the settlement and killed all the colonists. That massacre would be the only warfare between Native Americans and European colonists in Delaware.

In 1638, a group of Swedish settlers built Fort Christina near present-day Wilmington. They named the fort and a nearby river for the eleven-year-old queen of Sweden. The new colony, named New Sweden, also included settlers from Finland. The leader and first governor of the colony was a Dutchman named Peter Minuit. He had been dismissed as the governor of New Netherland (which included present-day New York). The Swedish colony continued to grow. By 1644, settlers from Sweden and

Celebrating a Rich Heritage

Each year, the Nanticoke people of Delaware host a traditional powwow—a Native American gathering. This event features singing and dancing, trading, and selling crafts and art, and other celebrations of Nanticoke heritage.

Finland were living on both sides of the Delaware River. The settlers made a permanent contribution to American life by constructing the first log cabins in America. American pioneers would build these simple structures for the next 250 years.

The Dutch knew that the Delaware River and Delaware Bay were important for trade and shipping. They wanted to gain control of the area. In 1651, they built Fort Casimir at the future site of the city of New Castle. The Swedes drove them out in 1654, but the Dutch stormed back and took over the fort and Fort Christina in 1655. Dutch control did not last long, either. In 1664, a powerful English fleet chartered by James, Duke of York and brother to Britain's King Charles II, sailed into Delaware Bay and quickly forced the Dutch to surrender.

William Penn addresses Swedish colonists in New Castle, where he landed upon his arrival in North America in 1682.

The Native People

For many years before the first Europeans arrived, the land of modern-day Delaware was home to small bands of Native Americans. The largest group was the Lenape, whom European settlers later called the Delaware. The Lenape lived in small villages close to the Delaware River and Delaware Bay. The men hunted and fished, and the women tended crops, prepared meals, and handled most of the childcare. A smaller tribe called the Nanticoke lived to the south and east, closer to Chesapeake Bay. The cultures of the Nanticoke and Lenape tribes are intertwined in many ways. While each group has their own region and way of living, they share many traditions and much of their history.

Both the Nanticoke and the Lenape relied heavily on farming to feed the tribe. Corn, beans, and squash were important crops for both groups. In addition, both the Nanticoke and the Lenape hunted animals such as bear, deer, turkeys, and geese. Each tribe used shells and beads in colorful traditional art and jewelry. The family unit was very important to both groups, as well, with strong ties being valued between parents and children.

European settlement had a significant impact on the history of both tribes. In 1684, settlers and Nanticoke reached an agreement to create a reservation in Maryland where much of the tribe could live. However, nonnative people continued to move onto this land, so in 1707 the Nanticoke purchased 3,000 acres (1214 ha) on the broad creek in Delaware. Continued resettlement eventually led to many Nanticoke moving to neighboring states and beyond. The Lenape faced similar trials, and many scattered across the eastern United States as a result of conflict with European settlers, intertribal fighting and disease.

Today, a small number of both Lenape and Nanticoke people remain in Delaware. The Nanticoke Indian Association of Millsboro has been a state-recognized tribe in Delaware since 1922. The last person speaking the Nanticoke language died in 1856. A large number of people from both tribes now live in Oklahoma, Pennsylvania, New Jersey, and parts of Canada. Though the Lenape population is largely diminished in Delaware, many who migrated to Oklahoma became part of the now federally recognized Delaware Nation.

Spotlight on the Nanticoke

In Algonquian, the common language of Northeastern tribes, the word Nanticoke means "the tidewater people."

Clans: The Nanticoke people were closely related to several tribes: the Choptank, the Assateague, the Piscataway, and the Doeg.

The Nanticoke are a tribe recognized by the state of Delaware.

Homes: The Nanticoke people built wigwams, dome-shaped homes made of wood, tree bark, and animal hide. Larger dwellings called longhouses were used for tribal gatherings.

Food: Farming was an important part of life for the Nanticoke. Corn, beans, squash, pumpkins, sunflowers, and tobacco were some of the crops they grew. They also gathered nuts and berries, and fished for clams, oysters, crabs, and more. Nanticoke men hunted small animals including ducks, geese, squirrels, and deer.

Clothing: Nanticoke people made pants, skirts and coats from animal hide and fur to survive cold winters. Decorations and jewelry were made from shells, beads, and feathers. Sometimes they used berries to tattoo or paint their skin.

Art: The Nanticoke created colorful jewelry, beadwork, and pottery. Like many other tribes, they made *wampum*, or beads made from shells.

Caesar Rodney rode overnight to cast his vote for independence.

In 1681, to satisfy a debt, King Charles II of England gave a huge tract of land to William Penn, who established the colony of Pennsylvania. However, the new colony did not have any waterways that led to the ocean. To solve that problem, the English gave Penn the land around the Delaware River. The area became known as the Lower Counties of Pennsylvania. The people in the three counties—New Castle, Kent, and Sussex—did not think they had enough say in the Pennsylvania government. In 1704, Penn agreed to let the Lower Counties set up their own assembly.

The town of New Castle became the capital of the Lower Counties. Today, a visual reminder of Delaware's unique history can be seen there. The New Castle Court House displays the flags of all four nations that controlled the area at different times—Sweden, the Netherlands, Great Britain, and the United States.

Between 1763 and 1767, surveyors named Charles Mason and Jeremiah Dixon drew the boundary that would become known as the Mason-Dixon line. The line's purpose was originally to settle a land dispute between British colonies in Maryland and Pennsylvania. The Mason-Dixon line became important again in the years leading up to and during the Civil War. It served as a symbolic marker between the states to the north that abolished slavery and those to the south where slavery remained legal. Today, the line is still referred to as a cultural boundary between the North and South.

Wilmington resident John Dickinson was called "the Penman of the Revolution." From 1767 to 1768, Dickinson published a series of essays called "Letters from a Farmer in Pennsylvania." The twelve letters were widely distributed among the thirteen colonies. The essays helped unite colonists against the Townshend Acts, a series of laws passed by the British in America that were met with great resistance by colonists. This backlash played a major role in the lead up to the American Revolution.

In Their Own Words

"Governments, like clocks, go from the motion men give them, and as governments are made and moved by men, so by them they are ruined too. Let men be good, and the government cannot be bad; if it be ill, they will cure it."

—William Penn, in Frame of Government of Pennsylvania, 1682

President Thomas Jefferson recognized Dickinson as being "among the first of the advocates for the rights of his country when assailed by Great Britain" whose "name will be consecrated in history as one of the great worthies of the revolution."

In July 1776, the Second Continental Congress met in Philadelphia to vote on the Declaration of Independence. There was no guarantee that the Declaration would be approved. Not all colonists wanted to break free from British rule. The two Delaware delegates in attendance were split. The third delegate, Caesar Rodney, was back in Delaware. When this news reached Rodney, he knew what he had to do. He rode through the night on horseback and arrived in time to break the tie in the Delaware delegation. Delaware voted for independence on July 2, and the Declaration of Independence was approved on July 4.

New Castle lawyer Thomas McKean also was an important voice in helping persuade the colonies to break away from British rule. McKean was one of Delaware's delegates to the First Continental Congress in 1774 and the Second Continental Congress in 1775. When McKean noticed Caesar Rodney was absent from the vote on the Declaration of Independence, he requested Rodney take his famous overnight ride to cast the deciding vote.

At the Stamp Act Congress of 1765, McKean proposed a voting procedure that would have a lasting impact throughout American history: that each colony, regardless of size or population, has one vote. The Congress of the Articles of Confederation also adopted the practice, and the principle of state equality continues in the United States Senate.

How to Make a Fishing Pole

Because of the state's beautiful coastline, fishing is a favorite pastime for many Delaware residents. Some like to fish off a pier at the beach or a riverbank, while others fish from a boat. Here are some instructions for making an inexpensive fishing pole of your own.

What You Need

Tree branch or bamboo rod—one inch (24 millimeters) diameter at the base and four or five feet (1.2–1.5 m) long (many garden stores sell bamboo).

Fishing line (available at sporting goods stores). You can also use kite string or dental floss.

Fishing hook (be careful with the sharp end!).

Bobber (or a cork wrapped with a rubber band).

A metal washer or nut to use as a weight.

What to Do

- Wrap the line a few times around the narrow end of the pole, and tie it with the same kind of knot you use to tie your shoe.
- Tie the hook on the free end of the line.

- Attach the bobber to the line about two feet (61 cm) above the hook (slip the line between the cork and the rubber band).
- Place the sinker between the hook and bobber.
- Find some bait and attach it to the hook. You can use earthworms or night crawlers you find outside. You can also use small pieces of bread, cheese, or even marshmallows. Be sure to ask an adult for permission before using any food.

Now you're ready to fish! Have an adult help you find a good place to fish. Some lakes and ponds are no-fishing zones to protect the animals that live in those waters.

You don't need a lot of money to enjoy fishing in Delaware.

Charles Wilson Peale's portrait of Thomas McKean and his son, Thomas McKean Jr.

In a way, Delaware's true declaration of independence had come a few weeks earlier. On June 15, 1776, the assembly had voted to separate from both the Pennsylvania colony and from English rule. The Lower Counties became known as Delaware State.

About four thousand soldiers from Delaware fought during the Revolution. However, only one brief battle was fought in Delaware, in September 1777. The battle took place in what is now the city of Newark. Only seven hundred colonial soldiers fought in the battle and the British easily fought them back and took control of the region.

Immediately after the battle, the British defeated George Washington's forces at Brandywine Creek, a few miles away in Pennsylvania. The British followed this success by launching a surprise attack against Wilmington and managed to capture the president (governor) of Delaware. The Delaware state government moved south from nearby New Castle to Dover for safety. Dover has been Delaware's capital ever since.

The colonies won their independence in 1783. A Constitutional Convention was held in Philadelphia in the summer of 1787. The new Constitution had to be ratified, or accepted, by the thirteen states. Each state held a special convention to debate and vote on the Constitution. On December 7, Delaware became the first state to approve it.

The Hagley Museum and Library is built on the grounds of DuPont's first gunpowder mill.

The 1800s

For much of its history, Delaware was mainly a farming state. The fast-moving streams and rivers provided waterpower for mills. These mills made Delaware an important center for processing flour and other foods that were sold in nearby cities, especially Philadelphia and Baltimore. In 1802, the du Pont family started a gunpowder mill on the banks of Brandywine Creek near Wilmington. The family founded the company just two years after fleeing France to escape the French Revolution. Throughout the 1800s and early 1900s, the DuPont mills produced most of the nation's gunpowder. The site of their original plant, called Eleutherian Mills, is now an expansive museum called the Hagley Museum and Library.

Trade and manufacturing gradually became more important to Delaware. The state's mills produced not only flour and gunpowder but also a variety of products, including cloth and paper. The city of Wilmington became a center for both manufacturing and trade. The methods for transporting goods in and out of Delaware improved. In 1829, the Chesapeake and Delaware Canal was opened. The canal reduced the water route from Philadelphia to Baltimore by nearly 300 miles (485 km). From the late 1830s on, railroads steadily grew in importance and water transportation declined.

In the 1860s, tensions between the North and the South led to the Civil War (1861–1865). Eleven Southern states broke away from the rest of the country and formed the Confederate States of America. One of the main reasons for the war was slavery. The first slaves brought to the British North American colonies

The Fight for Independence

By the 1770s, many people in the American colonies were calling for freedom from British rule. The colonists were tired of paying taxes to the British while having little say in how they were governed. They fought for their independence during the American Revolution [1775-1783]. Delaware played an important part in the revolution.

The DuPont family's first gunpowder mill was build along the Brandywine Creek.

Dover Air Force Base

Delaware Figure Skating Club

Smyrna

1. Wilmington: population 70,851

Delaware's most populous city is home to many kinds of businesses. Key industries that thrive in Wilmington include credit card companies, life insurance, banks, and legal services. DuPont, one of the largest chemical companies in the world, has its headquarters in the city.

2. Dover: population 36,047

The capital city of Delaware was a key stop on the Underground Railroad during the Civil War because of its location between Maryland, where slavery was legal, and the free states of Pennsylvania and New Jersey.

3. Newark: population 31,454

Newark is home to the University of Delaware Figure Skating Club, where some of the world's best figure skaters have trained. National, world, and Olympic champions, including some from other countries, travel to Newark to practice.

4. Middletown: population 18,871

Middletown is one of the fastest growing regions in Delaware. Between 2000 and 2010, the population of the town grew 206 percent. Every year, the town hosts the M.O.T. Big Ball Marathon to raise funds for charity.

5. Smyrna: population 10,023

This small town is rich in history. Smyrna was founded prior to the Revolutionary War, though it was originally called Duck Creek due to its location near the waterway of the same name. Shipbuilding, lumber, peaches, and grain were key industries in Smyrna's early days.

6. Milford: population 9,559

Milford was built along the Mispillion River. To celebrate the river's role in the town's history, Milford built the Mispillion Riverwalk, where visitors can stroll and see where seven shipyards produced more than six hundred wooden sailing ships between 1680 and 1927.

7. Seaford: population 6,928

In 1939, the DuPont Company chose Seaford as the site of the first nylon plant, leading to the moniker "Nylon Capital of the World." The region was also once the largest chicken-producing area in the world.

8. Georgetown: population 6,422

Every two years, Georgetown hosts a holiday known as **Return Day** two days after Election Day. The event originated in colonial days, when residents would gather in the town to hear election results. Winners and losers from political races still gather for this lighthearted celebration.

9. Elsmere: population 6,131

During the early twentieth century, the Delaware State Fair Association purchased land in Elsmere and built fairgrounds that included a racetrack for horses, cars, and motorcycles. This area became the site of the Delaware State Fair from 1917 to 1928.

10. New Castle: population 5,285

The area that would become New Castle was founded in 1651 by Peter Stuyvesant, one of the most notable leaders of Dutch settlement in the New World.

Milford

Return Day

New Castle

that became the United States had been kidnapped from Africa in the 1600s. By the mid-1800s, Southern farmers relied on slaves as field workers. However, most states in the North did not allow slavery.

Delaware struggled with the issue of slavery. In 1860, about twenty thousand free African Americans lived in the state. Many white Delawareans wanted to see slavery abolished, or ended. Some helped slaves on the Underground Railroad—a secret network of people who helped slaves escape to freedom in the years before the Civil War. Some Delaware homes and meeting houses served as "stations," or safe hiding places, for slaves on their journey north. Thomas Garrett was Delaware's most famous "conductor" on the Underground Railroad. Before the Civil War ended, he helped more than 2,700 slaves escape to freedom. He was arrested and fined in 1848 but he refused to give up his fight against slavery. Garrett was the inspiration for one of the main

Thomas Garrett guided thousands of slaves to freedom

Fort Delaware on Pea Patch Island is surrounded by a moat.

characters in *Uncle Tom's Cabin*, a book by Harriet Beecher Stowe that helped fuel the **abolitionist** movement with its antislavery message.

The general attitude at the time seemed to establish a pattern that New Castle County in the north was generally antislavery, and Sussex County in the south was proslavery. Several attempts were made to abolish slavery in Delaware. In 1792, lawmakers tried to make it part of the new state constitution, but failed. Bills to abolish slavery were introduced in the General Assembly in 1796 and 1797. In 1803, an attempt at gradual emancipation—slowly phasing slavery out—was ended by the speaker of the state House of Representatives, who cast the tiebreaking vote. Further attempts were made, but never passed.

Delawareans still owned about 1,800 slaves. Though Delaware stayed in the Union when the Civil War began, several hundred of its people fought for the Confederacy.

Masters of Materials

DuPont researchers developed many materials we use every day, including nylon (pantyhose), Mylar (used to make some balloons), and Kevlar (used in bulletproof vests).

After nearly four years of bloody battles, the Confederacy surrendered in the spring of 1865, and the country was unified once again. The Thirteenth Amendment to the U.S. Constitution officially abolished slavery nationwide in December 1865. Yet many decades would pass before African Americans in Delaware, and other states, would truly have equal rights.

After the war, large numbers of immigrants came to work in the factories in and near Wilmington. This allowed industry to thrive in Delaware. The southern part of Delaware maintained a strong agricultural economy, with corn and wheat being the main crops.

The Twentieth Century

In the twentieth century, industry changed in many ways—and the lives of Delawareans changed with it. The use of new sources of power, including steam and electricity, led to new industries in the Wilmington area. In addition to gunpowder, factories made ships, railroad cars, and machinery. These industries were important for America during World War I (in which the United States fought from 1917 to 1918) and World War II (in which the United States fought from 1941 to 1945).

Railroads gave farmers access to big-city markets.

Observation towers built in World War II are still standing on Delaware's beaches.

The Great Depression—a time of widespread economic hardship across the United States during the 1930s—had a great impact on Delaware's economy. Factories and businesses closed, leaving thousands of workers unemployed. However, Delaware suffered less than other states because of its strong agricultural industry.

Delaware's shoreline played an important role in World War II. Between 1939 and 1942, eleven observation towers were built on the coast of Delaware, in an area stretching 40 miles (64 km). Soldiers would man the guard towers for any sightings of enemy vessels. Because so many important sites of American industry existed in this area—chemical plants in Wilmington and Philadelphia's shipyard are two examples—it was considered a critically important area to protect.

These threats were very real, as German submarines sank U.S. ships off the East Coast and survivors of these attacks often ended up on Delaware's shores. One German submarine surrendered off one of the stations, Fort Miles, in 1945.

The towers were built to last twenty years, but some still stand today and are expected to last another half-century. Visitors can climb some of the towers, including the one at popular Cape Henlopen State Park, for spectacular views of Delaware and the Atlantic Ocean.

DuPont supplied much of the gunpowder used by Americans and their allies. The company continued to flourish in the early twentieth century and moved into manufacturing dynamite and smokeless powder. DuPont purchased several smaller chemical companies, and in 1912 these actions caught the attention of the U.S. government. The Sherman Anti-Trust Act was a federal law that barred companies from

Delaware women contributed to the war effort in the 1940s.

This original gunpowder wagon is on display at the Hagley Museum.

becoming anti-competitive—meaning they were so big that other companies were unable to compete against them. Under the act, the courts declared that DuPont had a monopoly, or unfair amount of control, in the explosives business and ordered them to split into smaller companies.

In spite of these challenges, DuPont continued to grow and established two of the first industrial laboratories in the United States. These are laboratories where scientists work to develop new products for a company to sell. The DuPont labs were key to the company's expansion into products that were not explosives.

In 1914, DuPont invested in General Motors (GM), helping the fledgling automotive company survive. Pierre S. du Pont, one of DuPont's owners, became president of GM.

Making Cents

Delaware kept up its tradition of being first in the nation when a commemorative quarter featuring the state helped launch the U.S. Mint's "50 State Quarters" program in 1999. The special quarter featured an image of Caesar Rodney on his overnight ride to Philadelphia to vote for independence.

In 1814, a religious festival called the Big August Quarterly was founded in Wilmington. It started as a quarterly conference for the African Union Church and became an opportunity for African Americans to gather and celebrate their heritage and faith. The event now features music, dancing, art, and children's activities.

Under his leadership, GM became the number one automotive maker in the world. In 1957, the U.S. Justice Department again ruled against DuPont, declaring that its investment in GM was considered a monopoly. The government forced DuPont to give up the large amount of stock it owned in the car company.

The increased production in factories and shipyards provided jobs for many Delawareans. While many men fought overseas, women in the United States served their country by working in factories and other industries that helped the war effort. Many Delawarean women worked at jobs that were available only to men before the war.

Delaware has continued to change since World War II. DuPont moved toward producing chemicals for paints and other household products. Most of the "heavy" industries have been replaced by "light" industries, which make such products as processed foods, medical instruments, and electronic components. Today, Delawareans try to continue to adapt to changing times.

10 KEY DATES IN STATE HISTORY

1. 1609
Henry Hudson sails into Delaware Bay and claims the entire area for the Dutch.

2. 1631
Dutch colonists set up the first European settlement in Delaware at what is now Lewes.

3. 1682
William Penn founds the Pennsylvania colony, which includes the three Lower Counties (modern-day Delaware).

4. June 15, 1776
Delaware separates from Pennsylvania and declares its independence from Great Britain. Just over two weeks later, Caesar Rodney rides to Philadelphia to cast Delaware's deciding vote for the Declaration of Independence.

5. December 7, 1787
Delaware becomes the first state to ratify the new U.S. Constitution. New Hampshire became the ninth state to ratify the constitution on Jun 21, 1788, making it the law of the land.

6. February 12, 1838
Railroads connect Philadelphia and Baltimore, encouraging industrial development in northern Delaware.

7. March 1981
Changes in state laws draw out-of-state banks to establish offices in Delaware. Many more banks and other business follow in the coming decades.

8. November 7, 2000
Delawareans elect their first female governor, Ruth Ann Minner. She served two four-year terms.

9. January 20, 2009
Delaware senator Joe Biden, the fifth-youngest senator ever elected when he won in 1972 at the age of 29, is sworn in as vice president of the United States, along with President Barack Obama.

10. October 29, 2012
Hurricane Sandy makes landfall along the East Coast, causing serious damage and flooding to parts of Delaware. Nearly 11 inches of rain fell at Indian River Inlet.

Delaware is a densely populated state.

The People

There are only five states with fewer people than Delaware. Those states are North Dakota, South Dakota, Alaska, Vermont, and Wyoming. Even though it is small, Delaware has a high population density, or number of people per square mile. The population density, in fact, is among the highest in the country. In 2010, Delaware had 460 people per square mile (sq. km), or sixth overall. The national average is about eighty-five people per square mile (sq. km). The state is far from crowded, however. Delaware's biggest city, Wilmington, has only about seventy-two thousand people.

Delaware has seen a remarkable mixing of people and cultures since the first Europeans arrived in the early 1600s. The original residents—the Native Americans—witnessed the arrival of settlers from the Netherlands, Sweden, and Finland, followed by England in the 1660s. In addition, small numbers of slaves were brought from Africa and sold to colonists.

According to 2010 U.S. Census Bureau estimates, nearly 69 percent of Delawareans are white. About 21 percent are black. More than half the population in Wilmington is African American. Asians account for 3 percent of the state population. Most of these people have

Much of Delaware's Hispanic population is proud to be from Puerto Rico.

roots in India, China, or the Philippines. Native Americans represent less than 1 percent. People who consider themselves Hispanic or Latino make up more than 8 percent of the state's population. Most of these people are of Mexican or Puerto Rican descent.

Native Americans

The makeup of Delaware's population changed a great deal during the 1700s. One change was the sharp decline in the Native American population. Many Lenape (later known as the Delaware) died from diseases brought by Europeans, such as **smallpox**. Much of the Native Americans' land was taken over by European settlers. Most of the indigenous people in Delaware moved west, joining other tribes beyond the Appalachian Mountains.

By 1750, only a few thousand Native Americans remained in Delaware. The Nanticokes, the only remaining group of the Delaware, live in central Delaware and number about five hundred people.

Delaware's Native Americans keep their traditions alive.

Immigrants from Europe

As the Native American population declined, the white population increased. The 1700s brought newcomers called the Scots-Irish; these people came from the area that today is known as Northern Ireland. In the 1800s, troubles in Europe brought two new groups. Starting in the 1820s, large numbers of immigrants came from Ireland, seeking to escape poverty. Immigration from Ireland increased further in the 1840s, when disease destroyed the potato crop—the main source of food for most poor families in Ireland. Large numbers of German immigrants arrived in the 1840s and 1850s, driven from their homeland by political unrest. Like many immigrants, both groups faced prejudice from many native-born Americans. By about 1900, however, both groups had melted into the mainstream of American life.

In the late 1800s, the development of industry, especially in and around Wilmington, drew a new wave of immigrants from southern and Eastern Europe. Poles, Slavs, Jews, Italians, and other groups arrived. They found work in factories and on the railroads.

Nancy Currie

Delino DeShields

Henry Heimlich

1. Emily Bissell

Born in 1861, Bissell founded Wilmington's first public kindergarten, and worked to introduce child labor laws in Delaware. Her most famous charitable project was the Christmas Seals program, which helped raise money for treatment and research of lung disease through the sale of seals, or stamps.

2. Annie Jump Cannon

Born in Dover in 1863, Cannon became an astronomer at the Harvard Observatory, where she gained fame for developing a system for classifying stars. It is still used throughout the world.

3. Nancy Currie

Currie is an engineer, United States Army officer and astronaut from Wilmington. Her spaceflight experience began in 1993 on the space shuttle Endeavor.

4. Delino DeShields

DeShields, a Seaford native, had a thirteen-year career as a second baseman in Major League Baseball. He finished in second place for the 1990 Rookie of the Year award with the Montreal Expos.

5. Henry Heimlich

Heimlich is a surgeon from Wilmington who developed the Heimlich maneuver in 1974. The maneuver uses upward thrusts on a choking person's abdomen to force the object out. Heimlich also invented a portable oxygen system called a Micro Trach.

DELAWARE ★ ★ ★ ★

6. William Julius "Judy" Johnson

Born in 1900, third baseman Johnson never got a chance to compete in baseball's major leagues. Before 1947, African Americans were mostly restricted to the Negro Leagues. The Wilmington native was elected to the Baseball Hall of Fame in 1975.

7. Thomas Macdonough

Born in what is now Macdonough, Delaware, in 1783, Macdonough gained fame in the wars against the Barbary Pirates (1805–1807). During the War of 1812, Macdonough captured a British fleet on Lake Champlain and saved New York and Vermont from invasion.

8. Ryan Phillippe

Born in New Castle, Phillippe's acting career spans more than two decades and includes film hits such as *I Know What You Did Last Summer*, *Gosford Park*, and *Flags of Our Fathers*. He also starred in the television show *Damages*.

9. Jeff Townes, AKA DJ Jazzy Jeff

Townes is famous for being a Philadelphia-born collaborator with actor Will Smith, but the DJ has made his home in Bear for the last several years. Townes also appeared on the television show *The Fresh Prince of Bel Air* as Smith's trouble-making best friend.

10. Johnny Weir

Olympic figure skater Weir grew up in Newark. Weir was a bronze medalist at the 2008 World Figure Skating Championships, a two-time Grand Prix Final bronze medalist, and three-time U.S. national champion.

Judy Johnson

Jeff Townes

Johnny Weir

Who Delawareans Are

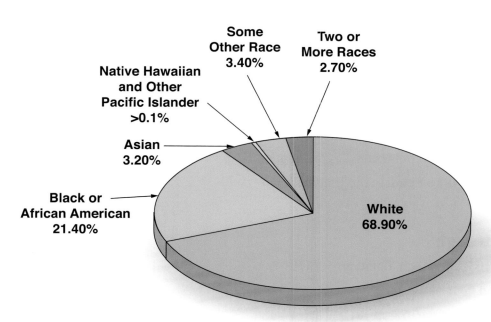

Some Other Race 3.40%

Two or More Races 2.70%

Native Hawaiian and Other Pacific Islander >0.1%

Asian 3.20%

Black or African American 21.40%

White 68.90%

Total Population 897,934

Hispanic or Latino (of any race):
- 73,221 people (8.20%)

Note: The pie chart shows the racial breakdown of the state's population based on the categories used by the U.S. Bureau of the Census. The Census Bureau reports information for Hispanics or Latinos separately, since they may be of any race. Percentages in the pie chart may not add to 100 because of rounding.

Source: U.S. Bureau of the Census, 2010 Census

A Mixing of Religions

The first European settlers represented different Protestant religions. The Dutch belonged to the Dutch Reform Church, and the Swedes were mostly Lutheran. Many English settlers were members of another Protestant group, the Episcopal Church. Small groups of Quakers also came to Delaware from Pennsylvania. Pennsylvania's founder, William Penn, was a Quaker. The Quakers were members of the Religious Society of Friends. Although few in number, the Quakers had a strong influence in Delaware. They strongly opposed slavery—in Delaware and in the rest of the United States.

The 1700s and 1800s saw the arrival of large numbers of Presbyterians and Roman Catholics. In the late 1700s, traveling preachers helped spread the beliefs of Methodism. The Methodist Episcopal Church soon became the largest in Delaware. Today, Roman Catholics and Methodists are the two biggest religious groups in the state.

Getting Around

Delaware's public transit system, called the "DART First State" system, was named "Most Outstanding Public Transportation System" in 2003 by the American Public Transportation Association. The system includes an extensive bus system and free or low-cost passenger rail and taxis.

Barratt's Chapel, built in 1780 in Kent County, is the oldest Methodist building in the United States.

Delaware After 1900

America's involvement in World War I and World War II led to a sharp increase in city populations, especially in Wilmington. Large numbers of people, including many African Americans from the South, came to work in the factories and shipyards.

After World War II, many people left Wilmington for its suburbs. Many newcomers to the state also moved to the suburbs. Today, about half of Delaware's people live within commuting distance of Wilmington.

Delaware experienced its largest population growth from 1950 to 1960. The continued development of the state's chemical industry drew scientists, technicians, and other workers from other parts of the United States and from other countries.

Most of southern Delaware remains rural. The area's population is also diverse—Kent County, for example, is home to prosperous dairy and potato farms operated by Polish-American families who moved from Long Island, New York. At Iron Hill, there is a large group of people from Finland who came after World War I. A small Amish settlement lies near Dover. The Amish people are a Christian sect. They live simply on farms and do not rely on modern machinery.

Working Together for Education

For many years, education was not unified throughout the state. While the early colonists valued education, most schools were operated by local churches, and the quality of the education was uneven. In about 1700, wealthy English families began sending their sons to schools in England. They educated their daughters at home or at boarding schools in Philadelphia.

Delaware established a fund for schools in 1796, but the money was not put to use for years. In 1829, a new law set up the state's first true public school system. Still, the quality of education in many schools was poor. Conditions were even worse for African American students, who were not allowed to attend the same schools as white children. In the 1920s, a member of the du Pont family donated a large sum of his own money to improve the schools. Much of the money went to build new schools for African Americans.

In 1954, the U.S. Supreme Court ruled that schools could no longer be segregated. All schools must be open to black students as well as white students. However, schools in some Delaware cities, especially Wilmington, did not want to change. In 1978, the city started a court-ordered program to integrate the schools. Black students from Wilmington were bused to schools in the suburbs. White students from the suburbs were bused to schools in the city.

Former First Lady Laura Bush reads to students in a Delaware school.

The University of Delaware, home of the Blue Hens, got its start more than 250 years ago.

The state continues to face educational challenges. For years, the average national test scores of white students have been much higher than those of black students. However, the 2009 results showed that African American students in Delaware are closing the gap faster than students in most states. That was a positive sign for the future of education in the First State.

Higher Learning

Delaware is home to two well-known public universities. Founded in 1743, the University of Delaware is the oldest college in the state. The Presbytery of Lewes sent out a petition that said there was a need for an educated clergy. The first class of the Rev. Dr. Francis Alison's new school included three men who would sign the Declaration of Independence: Thomas McKean, George Read, and James Smith. Read also was among those who signed the Constitution of the United States.

A women's college opened in 1914 and in 1921 it merged with the school founded by Dr. Francis and the two colleges became the University of Delaware.

About twenty thousand students are enrolled at the school. Delaware State University is a historically black college that was founded in 1891 and it has an enrollment of more than 4,500 students. Among its most famous graduates are trumpet player and composer Clifford Brown, football player and Super Bowl winner John Taylor, American diplomat Dr. Clyde Bishop, and astronomer David G. Turner.

10 KEY EVENTS ★

New Castle Court House

Delaware Kite Festival

1. Boast the Coast Maritime Festival

This October event in Lewes celebrates the importance of local marine life for Delaware. Activities celebrate the region's **nautical** legacy, leading up to a lighted boat parade on the Lewes-Rehoboth Canal. More than ten thousand people attend.

2. Day in Old New Castle

The oldest home and garden tour in the United States features walking tours to New Castle locations dating from the eighteenth century. This mid-May event has taken place for ninety years, and also features period music and reenactments.

3. The Delaware Kite Festival

On the Friday before Easter, hundreds of kites of every size and shape soar above Cape Henlopen State Park in Lewes during the Delaware Kite Festival. Competitors of all ages vie for awards in categories that include largest kite, youngest flyer, and highest kite.

4. Delaware Saengerbund Oktoberfest

You don't have to have German heritage to enjoy this September event in Newark. Traditional German food, live music and dancing by a Bavarian dance group, amusement rides, and an opening parade are included.

5. Dover Days Festival

Combining the best of Delaware's historical legacy with modern-day fun, this three-day celebration on the first weekend in May features parades, live music and entertainment, a maypole, historical reenactments, and residents dressed in colonial costumes.

6. Eastern Shore AFRAM Festival

Seaford is the host city for this August festival that celebrates the history and culture of African Americans in Delaware. The two-day event offers attendees music, pageants, traditional food, and more.

7. Old-Fashioned Ice Cream Festival

More than seventy-five thousand people attend this event each July in Wilmington. In addition to the opportunity to sample the state's best ice cream, the festival also features live music, fireworks, puppet shows, and more.

8. Punkin Chunkin World Championship

This pumpkin-throwing contest is held the first weekend after Halloween in Sussex County. Contestants create machines, including slingshots and catapults, to launch pumpkins thousands of feet. The event also features the Miss Punkin Chunkin pageant, and a pumpkin pie competition.

9. Separation Day

The people of Delaware celebrate their "first" independence day each June 15. On that day in 1776, the Delaware assembly voted to break free from the Pennsylvania colony and from Great Britain. Today, New Castle's weekend-long festival celebrates with live music and family-friendly activities.

10. Winterthur Point-to-Point

Point-to-Point is a steeplechase event, meaning competitors must jump fences and obstacles on the course. This May event is held at Winterthur, one of Delaware's most notable museums of American decorative arts.

Punkin Chunkin machine

Winterthur Point-to-Point

Bills are introduced and enacted
at Legislative Hall in Dover.

How the Government Works

The constitution of a state is its framework of government. Much like the U.S. Constitution, it describes the duties of the state government's three branches: the executive, the legislative, and the judicial. The executive branch, headed by the governor, runs the affairs of the state. The legislature makes laws. The judicial branch is composed of courts that settle disputes or hear cases when laws are broken.

During America's colonial period, the legislature in each colony could make its own laws, but the British monarch (the king or queen) could reject any law that he or she did not like. In 1776, when the Continental Congress approved the Declaration of Independence, the Thirteen Colonies became thirteen independent states and could write their own state constitutions. Delaware had a constitution ready by the end of 1776.

Over the next hundred-plus years, the legislature wrote three new constitutions. The state constitution in use today was written in 1897. However, Delawareans have added amendments, or made changes, to the constitution more than a hundred times. The process for amending the Delaware constitution is different from the process in any other state. The change must be approved by two-thirds of the legislature. The proposed amendment is then posted in newspapers in each county before the next election.

The legislature votes again. If the proposal again wins two-thirds of the vote, the amendment is officially added to the constitution. The governor cannot veto, or reject, a constitutional amendment.

Branches of Government

EXECUTIVE

The governor is the head of the state. He or she is responsible for approving or rejecting laws passed by the legislative branch. The governor prepares the state budget and suggests new laws. Along with the lieutenant governor, the attorney general, and the treasurer, the governor is elected to a four-year term. The governor is allowed to serve only two terms.

LEGISLATIVE

The general assembly makes state laws. It is divided into two parts. The twenty-one senators are elected for four-year terms. The forty-one members of the house of representatives serve two-year terms. There is no limit on the number of terms a member of the general assembly can serve.

JUDICIAL

All judges are appointed by the governor with the approval of the senate. These judges serve twelve-year terms. The highest court, the state supreme court, hears appeals from lower courts and can decide whether a law violates some part of the state constitution. Below the supreme court is the superior court, for criminal and civil cases. **The Court of Chancery** hears cases involving business disputes. The lowest courts hear cases involving matters such as family disputes or traffic offenses.

How a Bill Becomes a Law

As in other states, before a law is passed in Delaware, it must go through an established process. Most laws begin with a suggestion or an idea from a Delaware resident or a member of the state legislature. The proposed law is called a bill.

The Delaware state legislature is called the general assembly. Like the U.S. Congress, it has a senate and a house of representatives. A bill may be introduced in either the senate or the house. From there, it is assigned to a committee. The committee members examine the bill, hold hearings, or meetings, and may revise the bill. The committee can reject the bill and decide not to present it to the entire house. If the committee is satisfied with the bill, it is presented to the rest of the house.

Ruth Ann Minner served two terms as governor of Delaware, becoming the first woman to hold that office.

The bill is read to the house three times. After the second reading, legislators can revise or amend the bill. They usually debate the bill after the third reading. After the third reading and the debates, the legislators vote on the bill. If the bill is approved, it is sent to the other house. There, it goes through a very similar process. If both houses agree on the bill, it is then sent to the governor. If the governor approves the bill, he or she can sign it into law.

Law Bans Spanking

In 2012, Delaware became the first state in the United States to pass a law that banned parents from spanking their children. The bill, supported by state Attorney General Beau Biden, redefined child abuse as any act that causes pain.

The governor may also make changes to the bill and send it back to the general assembly. If the governor does not take any action, the bill will automatically become law after a certain amount of time. The governor can also veto the bill. A vetoed bill can still become law if two-thirds of the members of both houses vote to override the governor's veto.

Local Government

The counties—New Castle, Kent, and Sussex—are the primary units for local government. New Castle and Sussex governments consist of an elected council and council president.

Kent County uses an older system. It has an elected board of commissioners called the "levy court." The name comes from the old tradition of levying, or collecting, taxes.

In addition, Delaware's large towns and cities generally elect a mayor and a council. A few hire a city manager rather than a mayor. Near the state's northern border, three villages known as the Ardens do not have any official government. Citizens work together to solve problems in the villages. The Ardens operate according to the ideas of Henry George, an author in the late 1800s. The townspeople own the land together rather than individually.

National Level

Like all states, Delaware is represented in the U.S. Congress in Washington, DC. Each state elects two U.S. senators. Senators serve six-year terms, and they can be elected as many times as voters choose. Delaware's longest-serving U.S. senator was Joe Biden. He was first elected in 1972 at the age of 29. He served until January 2009, when he gave up his position to become vice president of the United States.

Joe Biden's oldest son, Joe III (called Beau), is also involved in Delaware politics. In 2006, Beau was elected state attorney general—the top law officer in the state. Beau is a member of the Delaware National Guard. He served in Iraq from 2008 to 2009 and kept his post as attorney general.

He served as attorney general for eight years but chose not to run again in 2014 because he planned to run for governor in 2016.

Delawareans elect one person to the U.S. House of Representatives. A state's population determines its number of representatives. In 2010, Delaware was one of seven states that

Beau Biden followed his famous father Joe Biden into political office in Delaware.

have only one representative. California has the most people and the most representatives of any state (53 in 2010).

Citizen Leadership

The people of Delaware have a history of using their own money to fund important state projects. In the 1820s, Delawareans knew that a canal to connect the Delaware River and Chesapeake Bay would be good for business. The canal would make transporting products cheaper and faster. They had seen how the recently completed Erie Canal across New York State had reduced the cost of shipping farm products by 90 percent. However, Delaware's general assembly had recently established a fund for schools, and there was not enough money left for a canal.

Business owners from Delaware, Pennsylvania, and Maryland decided to build the canal on their own. They raised money, formed a company, and built the Chesapeake and Delaware Canal. The 14-mile (22.5-km) canal was completed in 1829. With locks to raise and lower ships, the canal greatly cut the time needed to ship products from Philadelphia to Baltimore. In 1919, the federal government bought the canal and deepened it for ocean steamships.

A similar event took place in the early 1900s. The development of the automobile created the need for paved roads, especially running north-south. The farms and towns of southern Delaware were not connected to cities in the northern part of the state. But there was no money in the state budget to build the needed roadway. T. Coleman du Pont, a member of the state's famous business family, undertook the task with his own money in 1911. The DuPont Highway was completed in 1924. Du Pont then turned it over to the highway department as a family gift to the state.

These are bold examples of how residents can work together to improve their state. Delawareans do not have to be wealthy to make a difference. In 2009, a Wilmington high school student won a national award for her community service. She volunteered with Success Won't Wait (successwontwait.org), a program that gives books to disadvantaged students and adults. The program was started by a Delaware college student in 2002, Vincenza Carrieri-Russo, who became Miss Delaware. To date, Success Won't Wait has collected more than 500,000 books.

People can also get involved by calling, writing, and e-mailing their representatives in the state government in Dover. They can suggest new laws, discuss problems in their community, and work together to make Delaware a better place to live.

POLITICAL FIGURES
FROM DELAWARE

1. Joe Biden: Vice President of the United States, 2009-2017

Born in Pennsylvania in 1942, Biden moved with his family to Claymont, Delaware, in 1953. Beginning in 1972, he was elected to the U.S. Senate six times. As Barack Obama's running mate, Biden was elected the forty-seventh vice president of the United States in 2008, and reelected in 2012.

2. Jack Markell: Governor of Delaware, 2009-2017

Newark native Markell became Delaware's first Jewish governor when he took office in 2009. Previously, Markell was one of the earliest employees of telecommunications company Nextel. He was reelected to his second and final term in 2012 as Delaware limits governors to two terms.

3. William V. Roth, Jr.: Member of U.S. Senate, 1971-2001

Roth served two terms in the U.S. House of Representatives, then five in the Senate. He was coauthor of the Economic Recovery Act of 1981 with congressman Jack Kemp, and was the sponsor of a bill to create the individual retirement account that bears his name, the Roth IRA.

DELAWARE

YOU CAN MAKE A DIFFERENCE

Contacting Lawmakers

Is there an issue affecting your town, region or state that you feel strongly about? Contact Delaware's governor, members of the general assembly, or representatives in the U.S. Congress. To find the name of your local representatives, visit www.delaware.gov and scroll down until you find the section titled "Find Your Legislator." Once you know the name of your elected officials, visit www.delaware.gov/egov/portal.nsf/portal/elected. When you find your official's name, click on it. At the top of the page there should be a drop-down menu with contact information on how you can call, write, or e-mail your representative.

People Speak

Citizens of Delaware have many ways of participating in the lawmaking process, including contacting your local lawmakers to let them know the issues you care about.

One bill that created controversy in Delaware, and inspired many citizens to contact their elected officials, was House Bill 88. This bill proposed changes to Delaware's gun laws that would make it more difficult for those suffering from mental illness to obtain a gun. Medical health professionals would have been required to report to police when a mentally ill person spoke

National organizations voiced their opinions on House Bill 88.

or wrote of a threat of violence against themselves or another identified person and had the capacity to carry it out. It was a bipartisan bill, which means it had support from both republicans and democrats.

Some Delaware residents thought the proposed law was unfair, while others thought it was a good way of keeping citizens safer. National organizations on both sides of the issue voiced their opinions as well. Some even protested in public to express their opinion on the subject.

The bill was passed in Delaware's House of Representatives, but after much deliberation, it was defeated in the state senate on June 27, 2013.

A change in regulations brought corporate offices to Wilmington.

Making a Living

The morning mists rose above the streams and rivers of northern Delaware. As the sun glistened on the lapping water of mill wheels, the steady power of the water turned large stone grinding wheels. This quiet scene was repeated every day through the early 1800s. Farm wagons would drive up to the stone millhouses with loads of corn or wheat to be ground into meal or flour. Mills were also used for cutting lumber and for making paper and textiles. One of the early mills, established on the Brandywine Creek in 1802, was used to manufacture gunpowder.

The early settlers of Delaware built their farms and plantations close to the rivers and streams to make use of the waterways for transportation. There were few roads in Delaware until the 1900s, so transportation by horse-drawn vehicles was slow. Boats or sailing ships were more convenient.

In the colonial years, many of Delaware's farms and plantations grew tobacco. Ships picked up the product from the docks and transported it to markets in Europe. Tobacco rapidly wore out the soil, however, and Delawareans searched for new sources of farm income. Many in the northern part of the state turned to wheat. Corn became the major crop in southern Delaware.

Soybean farms, such as this one depicted in Sussex County, have become major contributors to Delaware's economy.

In the 1800s, the growing and selling of peaches created a great wave of prosperity for the state's farmers. The crops were shipped by the waterways. After 1840, they were sent by railroad to city markets, especially in Philadelphia and New York. Peach tree orchards in the state included more than 800,000 trees. However, the peaches were stricken by a **blight**, or disease, called the yellows, and the orchards declined steadily after 1900. Peach growing picked up after World War II. Today, Delaware growers produce about two million pounds (907,100 kilograms) of peaches each year.

Still Farming

The development of industry, beginning in the late 1800s, became a larger source of income, but farming has remained very important. As the peach orchards declined, many farmers turned to growing other fruits and vegetables. Crops such as beans, peas, tomatoes, berries, and melons were shipped by water or rail. Today these farms are called **"truck farms,"** since road transportation has replaced railroads and ships to move the farm products to market. Many truck farms are operated by part-time farmers.

Today, Delaware's farm industry continues to thrive. The state is home to about 2,500 farms that cover 500,000 acres (200,000 ha). Sussex County is one of the wealthiest agricultural counties in the country. Chicken broilers are Delaware's biggest farm product. Delaware farmers raise more than 250 million chickens for their meat. Yet this important industry started by accident. In the early 1920s, Cecile and Wilmer Steele of Ocean View ordered fifty chickens. They wanted to raise the chickens and sell their eggs. But when the Steeles received five hundred chickens by mistake, they decided to raise them for their meat. Delaware's broiler industry was born.

In addition to corn and wheat, soybeans have become a major crop. Farm families in the extreme south also make holly wreaths during the Christmas season. Dairy and cattle farms are also key parts of the farming economy.

Commercial fishing remains profitable, although pollution problems have reduced the number of fishing boats. Fishing boats and chartered boats are used to catch saltwater fish in Delaware Bay and the ocean. Shellfish harvesting along the coast is profitable as well.

The DuPont Story

One of the most important people in Delaware's history was an immigrant from Paris, France. Eleuthère Irénée du Pont de Nemours arrived in the United States in 1799. Three years later, he persuaded his father to finance the building of a mill to manufacture gunpowder. The high quality of the product made the company a great success. It rapidly became the country's largest supplier of gunpowder and one of the largest in the world.

Eluthère Irénée du Pont came from France to start DuPont, now a worldwide company.

★ 10 ★ KEY INDUSTRIES ★

Agriculture

Beach Vacations

Chemical Research

1. Agriculture

Delaware's bridges and roads have given families easy access to city markets. Truck farms in Kent and Sussex counties grow table vegetables, such as lettuce, tomatoes, broccoli, beans, peas, and squash. Cherries, peaches, and melons are among the many fruits grown on truck farms.

2. Beach Vacations

Rehoboth Beach and Bethany Beach are an easy drive from Pennsylvania, Maryland, New Jersey, and Washington, DC. In fact, Rehoboth Beach is sometimes called the Nation's Summer Capital because so many people from Washington, DC, take vacations there.

3. Chemical Research

In the late 1930s, the invention of nylon by DuPont scientists caused a sensation worldwide. This breakthrough in the development of synthetic, or human-made, materials led dozens of chemical companies to establish research laboratories in Delaware.

4. Chicken Farming

Raising chickens has become the largest source of agricultural income in the state. More than eight hundred Delaware farms raise chickens. Much of the corn and soybeans grown in Delaware is used as chicken feed.

5. Construction

With so much business booming in Delaware, it's no surprise that more than twenty-eight thousand people work in the construction industry here.

6. Education and Health Care

More than ninety-nine thousand Delaware residents are employed in the health care or education sectors, more than any other industry. The University of Delaware, the Christiana Healthcare System, and Bayhealth Medical Center are some of the top employers in the state.

7. Financial Services

Delaware's business-friendly laws have made it a favorite location for financial services companies to set up shop. These companies account for about 50 percent of the state's Gross Domestic Product.

8. Food Processing

This industry is the second largest in the state in manufacturing after chemicals production. Prepared desserts, chicken, soft drinks, and fish products are just a few of the foodstuffs processed or canned here.

9. Manufacturing

Manufacturers make many different kinds of products in Delaware, from traditional goods, such as women's clothes made by Playtex, to technical materials such as the chemicals made by DuPont or Rohm and Haas.

10. Museums

Delaware is home to many wonderful museums, including the Winterthur Museum near Wilmington, which is devoted to the decorative arts. In addition, entire sections of some towns, such as the Old Court House area of New Castle, are "living museums" of buildings from the 1700s and 1800s.

Education

Food Processing

Winterthur Museum

Recipe for Caramel Corn

Visitors to Delaware's beaches love to stop by the boardwalk for treats: ice cream, French fries, and especially caramel corn. This recipe is an easy way to make your own caramel corn using just a microwave and a few ingredients.

What You Need

4 quarts (4.4 liters) popped popcorn
1 cup (237 milliliters) brown sugar
½ cup (118 mL) margarine
¼ cup (59 mL) light corn syrup
½ teaspoon (2.5 mL) salt
1 teaspoon (5 mL) vanilla extract
½ teaspoon (2.5 mL) baking soda
Waxed paper

What to Do

- Place the popped popcorn into a paper bag or large bowl.
- In a large two-quart (1.9-L) casserole dish or other microwave-safe container, combine the brown sugar, margarine, corn syrup, salt and vanilla.
- Heat for three minutes in the microwave. (Ask an adult for permission and help first.)
- Take out of the microwave and stir the ingredients until they are blended.
- Cook in the microwave for another minute and a half.
- Remove from microwave. Stir in the baking soda.

- Pour the mixture over the popcorn in the bag or bowl. Shake or toss to coat the popcorn.
- Place the bag or bowl into the microwave and heat for one minute.
- Dump the popcorn onto the waxed paper and let cool until the syrupy coating is hardened.

Enjoy! Store the leftovers in a container with a lid.

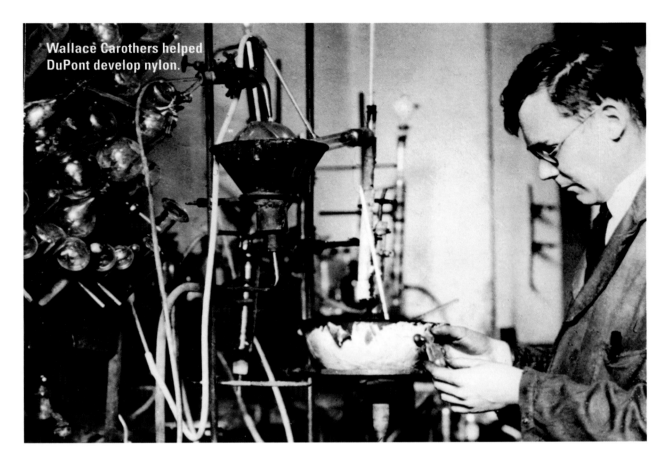
Wallace Carothers helped DuPont develop nylon.

Since the early 1800s, DuPont has been a mainstay of Delaware's economy. The family no longer owns the company. However, family members in each generation have been major figures in state culture and politics.

In 1912, the federal government ruled that the DuPont Company was a monopoly in the manufacture of gunpowder. A monopoly is a company that controls so much of an industry that it has no competition. As a result, DuPont was divided into three corporations: Atlas, Hercules, and DuPont.

In the early twentieth century, DuPont moved away from gunpowder production. The company began to focus on the development of chemical products, such as paint and dyes. In the mid-1930s, Wallace Carothers and other DuPont chemists developed nylon. This was a major breakthrough for the company. Nylon was used as a fabric to make parachutes and other products. Its most popular use was in women's stockings.

The DuPont laboratories and a manufacturing plant helped make Wilmington an important industrial center. The city has been called the "chemical capital of the world." The city's location is also ideal for business. Waterways, railroads, and highways place northern Delaware within easy reach of Philadelphia, Washington, DC, and other cities.

The Delaware Memorial Bridge speeds traffic into New Jersey and northward to New York.

Finding Work

There is much more to industry in Delaware than chemicals, of course. Food processing is a big part of the state's economy. Large plants in Dover, for example, make gelatin, puddings, and other dessert products. Other plants in northern Delaware make baked goods, fish products, and soft drinks. Poultry processing is also an important industry. The completion of the Delaware Memorial Bridge in 1951 linked Delaware with New Jersey. Major automobile companies soon set up assembly plants in Delaware.

Many farms across the state raise hogs. Hog farms sell their livestock to companies all over the state and throughout the country. Some of the livestock is sent to meat processing plants in Delaware. The hogs are used for ham, bacon, and other pork products.

Government is also a major source of employment. Many people have jobs in state and local government offices, in public school systems, and at the U.S. military's Dover Air Force Base.

For a small state, Delaware has a great deal to offer tourists. Visitors enjoy the state's beaches and the clear waters of the bay, rivers, lakes, and streams. The parks and forests are excellent for hiking, mountain biking, camping, and bird-watching. Others come to the state to see the historic sites that honor Delaware's—and the nation's—history.

One of the state's top attractions is Dover Downs. The complex includes a hotel, a casino, and a harness racing track. It is also home to Dover International Speedway. Each year, more than 135,000 fans pack the speedway to watch the top NASCAR drivers in action.

Delaware does not have any major sports teams, but it does have the Blue Rocks. The Blue Rocks are a minor league baseball team in Wilmington. Many future Major League stars played for the team, including Carlos Beltran, Johnny Damon, and Jacoby Ellsbury.

Festivals, fairs, and other events also draw people to Delaware. The state has a number of museums and galleries where people can admire art and other unique treasures. Visitors also love shopping in Delaware's outlets and other retail shops. The state is one of the few that has no sales tax.

Tourism in Delaware brings in money for the state and provides jobs for state residents. The steady growth of tourism creates a wide variety of jobs in service industries, including restaurants, hotels, and motels.

"The Home of Corporations"

During the 1970s, many Delawareans were out of work. Business and government leaders came up with an unusual solution. Lawmakers changed the state's business laws to attract out-of-state companies, especially banks and credit card companies. Dozens of corporations took advantage of the laws and set up corporate offices in the Wilmington area. Delaware got a new nickname—"the Home of Corporations." These companies created new jobs and brought extra tax income to the state. At the same time, the need for offices and housing contributed to steady growth in the construction industry. Today, thousands of banks and corporations have some connection to Delaware.

In 2008, the U.S. economy took a major hit. Millions of Americans lost their jobs, and countless businesses folded. The people of Delaware suffered along with the rest of the country. By the beginning of 2010, more than thirty-eight thousand people were out of work. Wilmington was hit the hardest. Nearly 13 percent of workers in the city were unemployed. The state's last two auto manufacturing plants shut down. State employees were forced to take a pay cut. Governor Jack Markell praised the people of Delaware for remaining strong during the tough times. "I remain firmly convinced that our state's best days are ahead of us," he said.

The state's unemployment rate has rebounded. It matched the national average in July 2014.

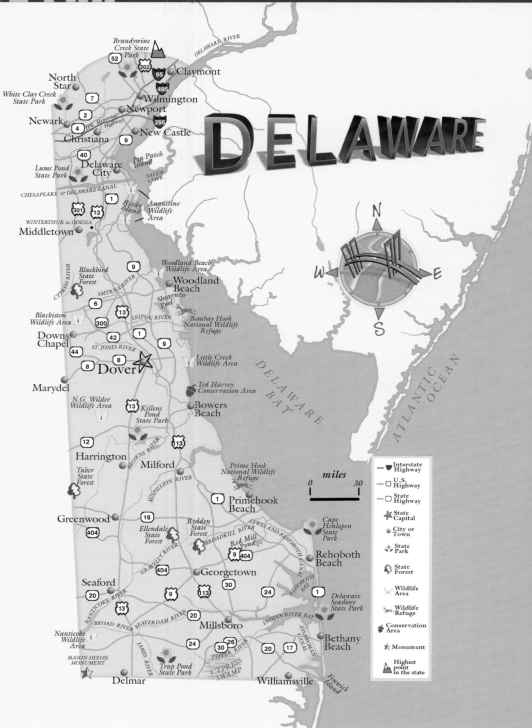

DELAWARE

Brandywine Creek State Park

52

202 95 Claymont

North Star

White Clay Creek State Park

7

495

Wilmington

Newport

2

Newark

4

Christiana

9

New Castle

295

40

Delaware City

Pea Patch Island

SALEM COVE

Lums Pond State Park

CHESAPEAKE & DELAWARE CANAL

301 13 1

Reedy Island

Augustine Wildlife Area

WINTERTHUR in ODESSA

Middletown

Blackbird State Forest

9

CYPRESS RIVER

Woodland Beach Wildlife Area

Woodland Beach

SMYRNA RIVER

Shearness Pool

6

Blackiston Wildlife Area

13

300

LEIPSIC RIVER

Bombay Hook National Wildlife Refuge

Downs Chapel

42

1

9

St. JONES RIVER

Little Creek Wildlife Area

44

8 8

Dover

Marydel

N.G. Wilder Wildlife Area

Ted Harvey Conservation Area

13

Killens Pond State Park

Bowers Beach

DELAWARE BAY

12

13

BROWNS RIVER

Harrington

Milford

Taber State Forest

MISPILLION RIVER

Prime Hook National Wildlife Refuge

miles

0   30

1

Primehook Beach

Greenwood

16

Readden State Forest

BROADKILL RIVER

LEWES AND REHOBOTH CANAL

Cape Henlopen State Park

404

Ellendale State Forest

Red Mill Pond

9 404

Rehoboth Beach

GRAVELLY RIVER

404

Georgetown

Seaford

20

30

Delaware Seashore State Park

NANTICOKE RIVER

9

13

24

1

13

REHOBOTH BAY

INDIAN RIVER BAY

Nanticoke Wildlife Area

BROAD RIVER

BEAVERDAM RIVER

20

Millsboro

ASSAWOMAN CANAL

Bethany Beach

MASON-DIXON MONUMENT

JAMES RIVER

24

30 26

PEPPER RIVER

20 17

CYPRESS SWAMP

Fenwick Island

Trap Pond State Park

Delmar

Williamsville

Legend:
- Interstate Highway
- U.S. Highway
- State Highway
- State Capital
- City or Town
- State Park
- State Forest
- Wildlife Area
- Wildlife Refuge
- Conservation Area
- Monument
- Highest point in the state

DELAWARE ★ ★ ★
MAP SKILLS

1. Which state park is located directly north of Rehoboth Beach?

2. How many wildlife areas can you count on the map?

3. How many different types of bodies of water are located in Delaware?

4. Which three Interstate highways intersect near Wilmington?

5. Which river is closest to the city of Seaford?

6. If you wanted to drive from Wilmington to Christiana, in what direction should you travel?

7. What is the name of the park closest to the highest point in the state?

8. What body of water, located south of Delaware City, cuts across the entire state?

9. What is the name of the conservation area located directly north of Bowers Beach?

10. The town of Milford is located on which river?

Cape Henlopen State Park

Ted Harvey Wildlife Area

1. Cape Henlopen State Park
2. Seven
3. Seven: river, pond, canal, bay, pool, swamp, and ocean
4. 95, 495, and 295
5. Nanticoke River
6. Southwest
7. Brandywine Creek State Park
8. Chesapeake and Delaware Canal
9. Ted Harvey Wildlife Area
10. Mispillion River

State Flag, Seal, and Song

The state flag is blue with Delaware's coat of arms (the image from the state seal) inside a buff-colored (yellowish) diamond. The date of Delaware's statehood is printed beneath the diamond.

Delaware's state seal includes the state's coat of arms in the center. The two men in the coat of arms are a farmer (to represent farming) and a militiaman (to represent liberty). The ox represents livestock, and corn and wheat represent agriculture. Water represents the Delaware River, and a ship represents shipbuilding and the coastal economy. Below these items is a banner with the state motto. Along the bottom of the seal are three years: 1704 is the year that Delaware's general assembly was established; 1776 is the year of American independence from Great Britain; and 1787 is Delaware's year of statehood.

The State Song is "Our Delaware," with words written by George Hynson and music composed by William Brown. To learn the lyrics, visit
www.50states.com/songs/delaware

Glossary

abolitionist   A person who wanted to ban slavery in the lead up to, and during, the Civil War.

belemnite   The state fossil came from sea creatures that are now extinct, but are believed to be related to squid.

blight   A disease, often one that affects plants.

Court of Chancery   A kind of court that focuses on cases involving business disputes.

global warming   The gradual increase in Earth's temperature.

Kevlar   A very strong material developed and trademarked by DuPont in 1965 that is used to make bulletproof vests.

nautical   Having to do with sailors, sailing, or other ocean-related activities.

peninsula   A strip of land jutting out into an ocean or lake from the mainland.

perennial   Plants that have a life cycle of more than two years.

Return Day   A tradition from colonial days that brings Delaware residents together in Georgetown to celebrate election results, including the winners and losers of the election.

smallpox   A viral disease that often involves a high fever and rash. Many Native Americans died from smallpox after Europeans arrived in North America.

truck farm   Farms, usually small, that produce vegetables and fruits that are transported by trucks to markets.

wampum   Beads used in traditional Native American art and jewelry made from seashells.

More About Delaware

BOOKS

Cheripko, Jan. *Caesar Rodney's Ride: The Story of an American Patriot*. Honesdale, PA: Boyds Mills Press, 2004.

Dubuois, Muriel. *The Delaware Colony*. Minneapolis, MN: Capstone Press, 2006.

Fisher, Sidney George. *The Quaker Colonies, a Chronicle of the Proprietors of the Delaware*. Whitefish, MT: Kessinger Publishing, 2010.

Weslager, C.A. *Delaware's Forgotten Folk: The Story of the Moors and Nanticokes*. Philadelphia, PA: University of Pennsylvania Press, 2006.

WEBSITES

The Official Website for the First State
www.delaware.gov

State of Delaware Kids' Page
www.delaware.gov/egov/portal.nsf/portal/kids

Family-Friendly Activities in Delaware
delawarescene.com

AUTHOR

David C. King is an award-winning author who has written more than forty books for children and young adults.

Brian Fitzgerald has been an editor and a writer of children's books for more than a decade.

Kerry Jones Waring is a writer, editor, and marketing specialist who lives in Buffalo, New York.

Index

Page numbers in **boldface** are illustratons

Index